How Do Virtual Assistants Work?

by M.M. Eboch

raintree

Raintree is an imprint of Capstone Global Library Limited, a company incorporated in England and Wales having its registered office at 264 Banbury Road, Oxford, OX2 7DY – Registered company number: 6695582

www.raintree.co.uk
myorders@raintree.co.uk

Edited by Leah Kaminski
Designed by Sara Radka
Original illustrations © Capstone Global Library Limited 2021
Picture research by Eric Gohl
Production by Kathy McColley
Originated by Capstone Global Library Ltd
Printed and bound in India

978 1 3982 0451 5 (hardback)
978 1 3982 0450 8 (paperback)

British Library Cataloguing in Publication Data
A full catalogue record for this book is available from the British Library.

Acknowledgements
We would like to thank the following for permission to reproduce photographs: Alamy: Andriy Popov, 42, Cayman, 19, Ellen Isaacs, 8, The Lightwriter, 15, Tribune Content Agency LLC, 44; Getty Images: Ethan Miller, 35, kimberrywood, 13, Stringer/Ron Case, 18, Stringer/Tom Harley, 21; iStockphoto: Daisy-Daisy, 5, 28, fizkes, 6, MachineHeadz, 9 (bottom), metamorworks, 32, RyanKing999, 17, selimaksan, 25 (bottom left); Newscom: Cover Images/Catolet, 9 (top), ZUMA Press/Florence Low, 22, ZUMA Press/Joan Cros, 29; Pixabay: Clker-Free-Vector-Images, cover (house icon), mcmurryjulie, cover; Science Source: Pasquale Sorrentino, 23; Shutterstock: ArnaPhoto, 45, Artram, 39, Charles Brutlag, 7, CHM3N, 31, CoinUp, 11, Eric Broder Van Dyke, 40, fizkes, 24, Flamingo Images, 37, GlebSStock, 33, Jay Yuan, 25 (top left), JHVEPhoto, 25 (top right), Julia
LIORIKI, background (circuit board),
30, Proxima Studio, 43, Romrodphoto
Wikimedia: GChriss, 25 (bottom right

Every effort has been made to contact
Any omissions will be rectified in subs

All the internet addresses (URLs) give
However, due to the dynamic nature o
sites may have changed or ceased to e:
regret any inconvenience this may cau
accepted by either the author or the p

Contents

Words in **bold** are in the glossary.

A new kind of assistant

Would you like to listen to music while you write an essay? Do you wonder how fast a cheetah can run? Do you want to relax with a joke? Are you chilly and wish the house was warmer?

What if you had someone to take care of all those things for you?

No, not a parent! An assistant.

An assistant helps with work. A scientist may have assistants to help with research. Usually, an assistant is a human being.

Today, we also have assistants on our computer devices. These programs are called **virtual** assistants or VAs. They can do many useful and fun things. VAs can answer questions and send messages. They can play music or check the weather.

A virtual assistant can help a lot. It might even seem like a friend.

Virtual assistants are controlled by voice recognition technology.

HIGH-TECH FACT

Computer assistants can have several names. They may be called **digital** assistants. They are also called AI assistants. AI stands for **artificial intelligence**.

CHAPTER 1
What are virtual assistants?

Computers are everywhere in our lives. Many phones and some watches contain computers. A calculator is a type of computer. Game consoles and some TVs are too.

But when is a computer device a virtual assistant?

Several competing companies offer different virtual assistants.

Alexa is the voice service created by Amazon. Some of the products it works with are the Echo and Echo Dot.

A virtual assistant includes a microphone. It can understand voice commands. Most have speakers so they can speak to you. You can tell a virtual assistant to do certain things, such as send texts or make phone calls. You can also ask VAs to add items to lists or calendars. They can set alarms and send reminders too.

Most computers have virtual assistants built into them. Tablets and smartphones do too. You can also get special devices that act as virtual assistants. These may look like small speakers. You can keep that type on a table or worktop in your home. If you have several of those devices, they all work with the same VA.

Android Auto pairs a phone's VA with a car's built-in screen.

A virtual assistant can connect to a car or a building. In a car, you control the VA through a smartphone. People in the car can use the VA to play music or check the news headlines. They can have the VA lead games such as 20 Questions.

Smart litter boxes make sure the litter is always clean for fussy cats.

A "smart home" attaches special devices to the lights, heating and more. A virtual assistant can control these devices. You might ask the VA to dim the lights while you watch TV. You can also buy special "smart" objects for your smart home. A smart litter box will sift waste. The Furbo dog camera lets you talk to your pet and shoot it treats using your smartphone. A smart bed cover will let you make your bed with a tap of the app.

Some VA systems let you buy multiple speakers. You can place one in every room of your home. No one needs to shout that dinner is ready. They can ask the VA to inform the whole house.

Siri is one popular VA. It is used on Apple devices.

Several companies make virtual assistants. You can buy a device with the company's VA built into it.

The VA Siri is on many Apple devices. It is on Mac computers, iPads, Apple TV and phones and watches from Apple. Siri links all a user's Apple devices.

The VA Bixby is on Samsung phones. Bixby works with other Samsung products, including smart home devices.

Samsung's VA is called Bixby.

The Amazon Echo is a stand-alone device. You keep it in your home. With it, you can order items from Amazon. It can also do other actions through its VA, called Alexa. Other Amazon products use Alexa as well.

Google Home is another stand-alone device. It uses the Internet search engine Google. This "Google Assistant" will also work on many phones and other devices. You can talk to it by typing in the Chrome web browser as well.

Google's VA does not have a human name. It's just called Google Assistant.

Why Alexa?

The name Alexa was chosen for a few reasons. Its *X* sound is unusual. That makes Alexa less likely to get confused with other words. Alexa is a reminder of the Library of Alexandria. This was a huge library in ancient Egypt. It tried to collect all the world's knowledge. The name Alexa suggests this assistant knows everything.

CHAPTER 2
How virtual assistants work

When you talk to a virtual assistant, you are really talking to a computer. A VA is always listening. You "wake up" the VA by saying its name or a keyword, something like "Hey, Siri" or "OK, Google". The VA starts waiting for commands or questions. This is a form of **voice activation**.

The VA connects to the internet. There, it can get information to answer your questions. It can follow your commands for online tasks, such as sending emails.

Every VA has been trained to **recognize** many words. This is called speech recognition or voice recognition. VAs may not understand every word. But they have learned how language works. Maybe the VA can't tell if you said *autumn* or *otter*. It can guess based on the rest of the sentence.

Virtual assistants also learn over time. They learn how people in general talk, and they learn how you talk.

The more you use them, the more VAs learn about your speech.

How does a computer learn?

Machine learning trains machines how to learn. You give a machine an example. It learns from that example. It can then take that knowledge to new areas.

Say you wanted to program a computer to play chess. You could tell it what to do when all the pieces are in a certain position. But chess is a complex game. There can be millions of different arrangements. A better way is to teach the computer the rules of chess. Then, let the program play thousands of games. Sometimes it wins. Sometimes it loses. It learns which moves are best at different times.

In 1997, a computer called Deep Blue was the first to beat a world champion at chess.

VAs learn in a similar way. Millions of people give their VAs commands. Sometimes, the VA does not understand. It may ask for more information. Or if it does the wrong thing, the user corrects it. Over time, the VA learns how people speak and what they mean.

Self-driving cars will contain virtual assistants that help the drivers easily interact with the cars' functions.

VAs work hard to understand us. You can help by speaking clearly and being specific about what you want. Say you have a smart home run by Alexa. You might say, "Alexa, turn on the light in bedroom one". Or you could say, "Hey, I'm going to my bedroom, so turn on some lights, Alexa". Which do you think will work better? Why?

If the VA can't understand you, it may ask you to repeat yourself. It might also ask for more information. Perhaps you ask it for a recipe for soup. It might then ask what kind of soup you want to make. Maybe you ask it to call Holly. But you have two friends called Holly. It will ask which one you want to call. As you use the VA more, it gets better at understanding. It's like a young child who learns more words and how to use them over time.

HIGH-TECH FACT

VAs correctly understand speech at least 95 per cent of the time. That's about the same as humans.

As software advances, talking to a VA is becoming more and more like talking to a human.

Intelligence

Something intelligent can gain and use knowledge. Intelligence takes many forms. The ability to understand speech. Translating one language to another. Making decisions. In computers, this behaviour is called artificial intelligence. AI is the science of helping machines copy human abilities.

CHAPTER 3
Virtual assistants grow up

Voice recognition is the key to VAs. This technology got its start over 70 years ago. Bell Laboratories built a machine called Audrey in 1952. It understood the numbers zero to nine.

In 1961, IBM, one of the earliest computer companies, built a system that could handle words. It recognized a whopping 16 words. Well, we all have to start somewhere. This showed that the idea was possible.

In the 1950s, voice recognition computers focused on understanding numbers.

Talking dolls

"Talking" dolls were being made by 1890. These dolls simply played a recording. In 1987, Worlds of Wonder released "Julie". This doll could recognize a few words and phrases. She knew how to respond. Julie also sensed light and motion. If you turned on the light, she might say, "Oh my, it's bright".

Master inventor Thomas Edison created one of the earliest talking dolls.

The 1970s brought big breakthroughs in technology. A program could understand over 1,000 words. That's about as many as a 3-year-old child knows. The program could understand words put into short phrases.

Computer systems learned more words and understood different voices. This made them more useful. Some businesses started using voice recognition. People could speak instead of type.

You could not talk normally with these programs. They had to hear each word by itself. That meant you had to pause after every single word. You . . . talked . . . like . . . this.

It wasn't easy to teach a computer human speech. Programmers wrote computer code to turn sounds into numbers. They spoke to a microphone attached to the computer. The computer turned these audio waves into numbers. The computer stored the numbers. The program matched each number to a specific word.

Later, a user might speak the same sound. The machine compared the new audio waves to the old ones. It looked for a match. If it found the same sound, the computer used the word that went with that number.

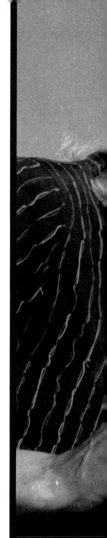

IBM created a new system in the 1980s. It knew about 20,000 English words. It even understood some full sentences. This new system needed each user to train it for 20 minutes. That helped the system learn how that person spoke.

Microphones were large and external in the early days of voice recognition.

Users still had to speak slowly and clearly. But the new method didn't simply match new sounds to old ones. It looked at patterns. It assumed people tend to repeat the same things. If it found a familiar pattern, it could predict what might come next.

More big changes came with a company called Dragon. They sold a speech recognition program in 1990. It cost £6,800. That's a lot for a computer program!

Dragon released a better program in 1997. Users no longer had to pause between words. They could speak naturally. The program was called Dragon NaturallySpeaking. It was much cheaper, though still not cheap, at £525.

Microsoft also worked on speech recognition. Its Windows computer programs added it. But many users didn't even know the option was there.

At first, users had to train Dragon for 45 minutes to understand them.

In the early days, these systems simply turned speech into text. You could speak and get words on the screen.

These programs did well with words they knew. But they didn't know every word. They also struggled with words that sounded like each other. *Can* might become *can't*. *You said* might become *used a*. For years, speech recognition was only about 80 per cent accurate. That meant correcting a lot. Often, it was easier to simply type.

In the 1990s, voice recognition software was used only on desktop computers.

I *will* help you

Microsoft introduced Clippy in 1996. Clippy looked like a paperclip with big eyes. It popped up on screen to offer help. The problem was, Clippy didn't wait for you to ask for help. People got annoyed when he interrupted their work. Clippy taught a valuable lesson. Virtual assistants should be quiet until someone asks for their help.

Once voice recognition was available on smartphones, the technology took off.

Speech recognition took another big leap with smartphones. People had a hard time typing on their tiny keyboards. Speech recognition made mistakes, but so did typing on a phone.

Google made a Voice Search app for the iPhone. Google gathered examples of speech. The app connected to the internet. That let it use **data** stored online. It could try to match the speaker's words to all those other examples. It wasn't limited to the data stored in that computer. The internet gave Voice Search more power than most programs.

Google added Voice Search to other phones and to an internet browser. It gathered more and more words from searches people made. It now has billions of words stored and is called Google Assistant. It is on over 1 billion devices, most of them smartphones.

Other companies made voice-recognition apps too. They got better and better. Today, VAs are part of daily life for many people.

VOICE RECOGNITION TIMELINE

1952 Bell Labs releases Audrey, which only understands its inventor.

1962 The IBM Shoebox recognizes 16 words.

1971 Harpy, from Carnegie Mellon University, understands over 1,000 words.

1996 Microsoft introduces Clippy.

2011 Siri, the first voice-enabled VA, is announced by Apple.

CHAPTER 4

What virtual assistants are doing today

In the last 10 years, VAs have become common. Speech recognition is highly accurate. Virtual assistants have also gained personality. You can change the voice your VA has. Choose female or male. Choose the accent.

You might not know what to do with a VA at first. Over time, you'll find many uses. You could get it to set your morning alarm with bouncy music to help you wake up. The VA can message a friend and ask him or her to meet you. The VA can check the weather and warn that you need a raincoat. It can remind you to pack your lunch.

Google Assistant had 10 different voices available in 2019.

No feelings

A VA is not a person. It cannot think or feel. Still, many people think of a VA as almost a friend. The companies that make the VAs want us to do that. You'll use your VA more if you think it's a friend you trust.

VAs are part of ambient computing, a system where devices around us constantly sense our needs.

Some VAs let you set up shortcuts. You say something like, "OK, Google, good morning". That tells the VA to do several things. It might switch on lights, check the weather and play music.

HIGH-TECH FACT

A 2018 study tried to learn which VA was smartest. At that time, Google Assistant won. It recognized and correctly answered the most questions.

What would you want a VA to do at different times of the day? What might a VA do for you in the future?

After school, your VA can order more stationery for school online. (First, make sure an adult says it's all right for you to order things!)

VAs can look up information and even solve maths problems on their own.

Then, your VA can help with your homework. Be careful, though. A VA can look up information. But is that information always correct? The VA simply searches the internet. Not everything on the internet is true. Also, VAs may find lots of facts but not tell you which fact is most important. A VA can help with homework, but it can't do it for you. Sorry, but you are still responsible for your own answers!

Jibo was specifically designed to be loveable.

You may also wonder about things that worry or scare you. Learning more facts doesn't always help. Say you're being bullied. Learning facts about bullying probably won't make you feel better. A hug might. When you're sad, scared or worried, talk to an adult. Adults can help you decide what to do. People can understand emotions. A VA can't.

Jibo

Jibo is a cute little robot. He was one of the first VAs. Jibo was supposed do all the things a VA can do. But he also had a personality. He danced and started conversations with his owners. The company that made Jibo shut down because his VA programs weren't useful enough. There may be a future where robots such as Jibo can help VAs seem warm and friendly.

If you only speak one language, you tell your VA what language to use. Simple! But do people in your house speak more than one language?

Google Assistant lets users set up two languages to use. Perhaps you set up English and Spanish. Then you can speak in either language. Google Assistant will answer in the same language. **Computer engineers** worked hard to make this happen. They hope to let people use three languages on a device one day.

You can speak to Google Assistant through the Google Home device.

HIGH-TECH FACT

Google Assistant can speak to users in about 20 languages. It will add more languages over time.

dating
Vitamy 歡迎 स्वागत आहे Welkom
Ласкаво просимо
benvenuti ꠆ پخیر **Bienvenue**
Aloha সুস্বাগত நல்வரவு
Velcome ברוכים הבאים Xush kelibsiz
ng Bine ați venit **Hoş geldiniz** សូមស្វាគមន៍
ожаловать! സ്വാഗതം أهلا و سهلا
Sannu da zuwa Ẹ ku abọ ようこそ
خوش آمدید HOAN NGHÊNH
Fáilte স্বাগতম Karibuni
envenidos wilujeung sumping ยินดีต้อนรับ
en ਜੀ ਆਇਆਂ ਨੂੰ। **bem-vindos**

You can use Google Assistant on your smartphone to translate about 44 languages into English.

Why is this taking so long? Think about it. You know when you hear another language. You may not know what language it is, though. How can a computer tell what language it hears?

The computer listens to the different sounds a voice makes. It listens to the voice's rise and fall. These give clues to the language. Once the VA has decided what language it's hearing, it can follow commands in that language.

Virtual assistants bring many good things to our lives. But they also cause worries about **privacy**. A VA is always learning. Companies use data coming from them to teach the VA. This information should not be connected to your name. Still, some people don't want a device to keep their messages and questions.

A VA may also record pieces of conversation. It should do this only after you wake it up. But sometimes, **software** doesn't work properly. It may record when you don't know it's on.

A VA like Alexa is always listening, but it does not record most of what it hears.

Hackers are a danger too. These criminals try to break into computers. They might spy on you and steal information.

What should you do to stay safe? Talk about it with your family. You can **mute** or turn off your devices when you don't need them. You can erase old recordings. Some device settings let you limit what is saved. You can also insist technology companies protect privacy.

Hackers can hide VA commands in white noise or music.

VAs fighting crime

Sometimes, crimes happen in people's homes. Was a virtual assistant listening? The police have asked for recordings from VAs. They have hoped to find evidence of crimes. Companies fight giving the police these recordings. They know customers value privacy. Which do you think is most important, privacy or fighting crime?

CHAPTER 5
Virtual assistants do odd jobs

VAs can do a lot in our homes. They can help at work too. VAs help workers set reminders and track their tasks. The VA can send messages while someone's busy doing something else. It can search thousands of documents quickly.

Many business websites offer a chatbot to customers as soon as they open the page.

A **chatbot** might be considered a type of VA. A company such as a hotel installs a chatbot. Customers can use the chatbot online. Hotel guests can check in, order room service or learn about local events. The chatbot works all day and night. The hotel doesn't need as many employees.

VAs can do tasks for all sorts of people. Radar Pace sunglasses are for athletes. They have a voice-activated system that combines a phone and a fitness tracker. You can make or answer a phone call while running. You can ask the VA about your heart rate and hear the answer. It even acts as a coach to help with training goals.

Radar Pace sunglasses aren't really "smartglasses". They use hearing, not sight, to coach runners.

VAs work in some special fields too, such as healthcare. A doctor's office VA might send reminders for appointments. The VA may help you fill out forms. It can help you order more medicine. Some medical VAs even offer advice online.

VAs can help doctors avoid mistakes too. Some hospitals use a VA to track patients' health issues and medication. Doctors give the VA instructions. The VA asks follow-up questions. How much medicine? How often should the patient take it? The VA looks for possible problems. If the prescription looks OK, the VA sends it in. With this VA, can reduce errors.

VAs cannot replace doctors and nurses. We still need humans. But VAs may save clinics time and money and help patients get better.

In the UK, Alexa is authorized to give certain medical information to users.

CHAPTER 6
The future of virtual assistants

Experts think virtual assistants will be used even more in the future. VAs help workers do their jobs. They help people control their homes.

Millions of people talk to their VAs every day. That provides billions of words to help the VAs learn. The VAs will keep learning more words and languages. They'll adapt better to accents. They'll be able to hear you even with noise in the background.

HIGH-TECH FACT

Some people work from home helping people with various tasks. Their job title is virtual assistant because they are assistants who work online.

Voice recognition is close to 100 per cent accurate in some languages. Can VAs ever be 100 per cent accurate? Do you think that is possible?

Some experts think that in a few decades, VAs will feel like an extension of ourselves.

VAs will also get faster. Most connect to the internet for speech recognition. They need all the speech records stored online. In the future, that data will be stored on each device. You won't need internet access. A phone will recognize words the instant they're spoken. It will work even in "aeroplane mode".

Virtual assistants rely on voice recognition. That's hard for people who can't hear or speak well. New VA features will help.

Google's Live Caption shows text for any speech playing on the phone. That lets people with hearing problems read the text from videos. Amazon has the smart speaker Echo Show. Its "Tap to Alexa" lets hard-of-hearing users tap common commands. They can read Alexa's responses with Alexa Captioning.

The Amazon Echo Show lets you type, rather than speak, commands. It can also recognize household objects that you place in front of its camera.

Virtual assistants help people with special needs in many ways.

If people can't speak clearly, a VA might not understand them. A Google product called Euphonia will help. It lets voice recognition learn a specific user's voice.

HIGH-TECH FACT
In the UK, about 2.5 million people have trouble with their speech.

A company called Voiceitt is working on a different app. The user will spend an hour or two reading short phrases. This creates a special dictionary with the user's voice. Then, the user can say those phrases and the VA will understand. Other companies may add new ways of helping people with special needs.

A VA can act as a hub for you to control your entire smart home.

Today, most people use VAs on their phones and computers. The future will bring more **stand-alone** smart home devices. Many families will get several home devices. They'll want them in the living room, kitchen and each bedroom. It is believed that in the near future, 85 per cent of customer services will be dealt with via chatbox and not humans.

For now, most smart speakers are small devices placed somewhere. Soon, they will simply be included in the things around us.

Many household objects will be tied to these VAs. The fridge. The oven. The washing machine. The dishwasher. Robot vacuum cleaners. Voice activation will control all these items.

VAs will even enter our bathrooms. A smart mirror adjusts the lights and plays music. The bath heats water to the temperature you like. The toilet plays music, turns on colourful lights and warms the seat. VAs will truly be everywhere.

The Roomba robot vacuum can be controlled via Alexa.

VAs make our lives easier. Some have so much personality they might seem like friends or family. They do raise concerns, though. What about privacy? Are there risks in computers doing so much for us?

Some people worry about children growing up with virtual assistants. Will children expect immediate answers to every question? Because Siri and Alexa don't have feelings, will children be rude? Even worse, will they stop talking to other people because they have VAs?

You can even play games with VAs. As they become more common, will they become part of the family?

Studies show that how VAs and chatbots are programmed affects people. If the AI is rude or selfish, people behave that way too. If the AI is friendly and cooperates, people respond that way. How could this be used, for good or for bad?

VAs bring some questions and challenges. They are still a growing part of our expanding virtual world. Soon, you may wonder how anyone lived without them.

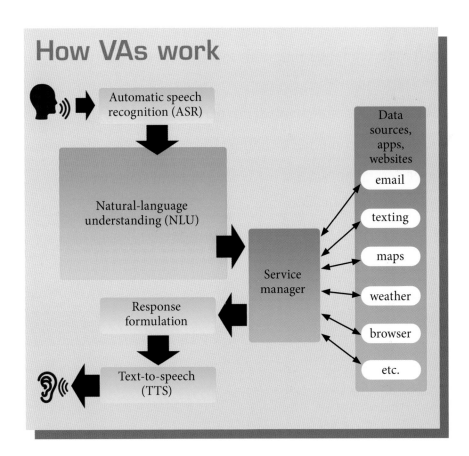

How VAs work

Automatic speech recognition (ASR)

Natural-language understanding (NLU)

Service manager

Response formulation

Text-to-speech (TTS)

Data sources, apps, websites
- email
- texting
- maps
- weather
- browser
- etc.

GLOSSARY

artificial intelligence ability of a machine to think like a person

chatbot computer program that talks with people using AI

computer engineer someone who designs computer software and hardware

data information processed or stored by a computer

digital electronic devices, especially computer technology

mute make silent; a mute button on a device cuts off the microphone

privacy being out of sight and hearing of other people

recognize know and remember

software computer programs made of lines of instructions for the computer

stand-alone self-contained, not part of something else

virtual on a computer or online

voice activation when a piece of equipment starts working when a person speaks

FIND OUT MORE

BOOKS

Artificial Intelligence and Work (The World of Artificial Intelligence), Alicia Z. Klepeis (Raintree, 2020)

Artificial Intelligence at Home and on the Go (The World of Artificial Intelligence), Tammy Enz (Raintree, 2020)

Robot: Meet the Machines of the Future, DK (DK Children, 2018)

Robots (DK Findout!), Dr Nathan Lepora (DK Children, 2018)

The Big Book of Invisible Technology: A Look at How Things Work for Kids, Chloe Taylor (Rockridge Press, 2020)

WEBSITE

www.bbc.co.uk/newsround/49274918
Find out more about AI with BBC Newsround.

INDEX